Kindly donated by the PTFA.
June 1990

Chasetown Primary School
Staffordshire

EXPLORING THE PAST

EXPLORING
BUILDINGS

Ralph Whitlock

Wayland

Exploring the Past

Exploring Buildings
Exploring Clothes
Exploring Farming
Exploring Industry
Exploring People
Exploring Transport

Series editor: Stephen Setford
Designed by: David Armitage

First published in 1987 by
Wayland (Publishers) Ltd
61 Western Road, Hove
East Sussex BN3 1JD

British Library Cataloguing in Publication Data
Whitlock, Ralph
  Buildings. – (Exploring the past)
  1. Architecture – Great Britain –
  History – Juvenile literature
  I. Title   II. Series
  720'.941   NA961

  ISBN 1–85210–002–8

Phototypeset by Kalligraphics Ltd, Redhill, Surrey
Printed in Italy by
G. Canale & C.S.p.A., Turin
Bound in the U.K. by
The Bath Press, Avon

Cover picture: In the Middle Ages, the Suffolk town of Lavenham was a centre for the wool industry.

Contents

1 Exploring the past

Why should we want to explore the past? Will we find it interesting to know what people did and how they lived many years ago?

The past, however, need not simply be many hundreds of years ago. It can be last week, or even yesterday. Can you remember what you were doing last weekend? Write down what you did. Now re-read what you have just written. That is the past – you have been writing history.

Supposing you start to make a model of a modern aeroplane. Then you put it in a cupboard and forget about it. The next time you see it is in twenty years' time, when you move house. When you find it again, you will be looking at history.

You would almost certainly be struck by how old-fashioned the model aeroplane looks. That is because designs change a lot in twenty years. Change is happening all the time. We can read

Notice the different building styles in this street in Tewkesbury. Look at the buildings in your neighbourhood or town centre. If they are mostly shops, look at the upper storeys as well as the shop fronts. You will probably see a variety of styles: some recent, some from earlier this century, and some even older.

A picture of stone-masons at work in the Middle Ages. Notice the tools and equipment they are using. Can you work out what each item is for?

about changes and we can also study them for ourselves, by looking at things people made in the past.

This book is about buildings. We spend our lives surrounded by buildings: houses, flats, shops, factories, football grounds and so on. Yet most of us take very little notice of them. All buildings belong to the past — even those that were finished only yesterday. We can learn a great deal by looking at them, no matter where we live. We can compare newer ones with those built many years ago. They will show us how ideas about building developed.

A modern building site. Compare this picture with the one above. Think of all the materials and equipment that are available today, but were not in the Middle Ages. Does this mean that all buildings today are much better than those built in the past?

5

2 Starting at home

If a building is going to be of any use at all when it is erected, it needs to be well-planned beforehand. Architects have to design the building, draw up detailed plans and say what materials are to be used. Here, an architect is drawing scaled plans for a house.

Look at a building you know well. It could be your home or even your school. Draw a picture of it. Can you draw a ground plan of the building as well? If your building has two storeys, you will need to draw two plans: one for the rooms downstairs and one for those upstairs. You may like to colour the parts of the building according to their use, or label each room and passage.

The people who built this building had to draw a plan first, before starting work on the site. They needed to know the size of each room so that they could buy the right quantities of bricks, concrete, timber and other materials. They had to know where electricity cables, water and gas pipes were to enter the building, and they had to allow for waste water to drain away.

How did they do this without having a sheet of paper as large as the house? The answer is that they worked to a scale. They may have decided that everything on the plan would be one-twentieth of its real size. Or they may have decided that every measurement of one metre would be represented by one centimetre on the plan. Whatever scale they chose, every measurement on the plan would have to conform to it. Have you ever tried drawing to scale? Start now, by drawing a plan of your bedroom or classroom on a scale of one centimetre to the metre.

After the builder had finished, whoever occupied the house would also have to consult the plans. They needed to know where all the pipes and cables were, so that they didn't bang nails into walls at the wrong places.

OFFICES
HOUSES
CINEMAS
SHOPS

Other kinds of buildings

Houses and schools are just two types of buildings. What others can you think of? Look around your own neighbourhood. Are there shops, offices, public houses, civic buildings, churches and other places of worship? Are there bus, railway or underground stations? Draw a plan of your neighbourhood, to show how they all fit in.

Work out a code of colours for your map. For instance, you could use blue for shops, red for private houses, yellow for offices and so on. Do they form a pattern on your plan? Keep this plan for future reference.

Above and below You probably think that you already know your neigbourhood well, but by the time you have listed the buildings in your area and mapped it out in detail, you may be surprised at how many different kinds of buildings there are.

3 Building materials

What are the buildings made of in your area? In modern buildings, reinforced concrete may be the chief material. In the past, builders used the materials that were most readily available. For instance, when Britain was covered with forests, houses were built of wood, just as the early settlers in America and Canada built log cabins to live in.

If stone was available simply by digging, they built stone houses. Stone is a very satisfactory building material and lasts a long time. At Skara Brae, in the Orkney Islands, people in Neolithic times (about 5,000 years ago) built houses entirely of stone because there were no trees on the islands. The walls were nearly two metres thick and each hut was equipped with stone benches, beds, basins and other stone furniture.

There are many areas, though, where there is no stone under the soil. Often there is clay instead, and this clay is shaped and baked into bricks. London is built chiefly on clay soil around the River Thames, so most of the early houses in London were made of baked clay bricks.

In places where building materials of any sort were scarce, people in early times often built houses of woven branches (called hurdles or wattles) plastered with mud or clay. This method of building is known as wattle and daub.

Does your part of the country have its own particular style of building? Are the older buildings built with a certain type of stone or wood? Are the roofs covered with slate or thatch? You can see some local building styles opposite.

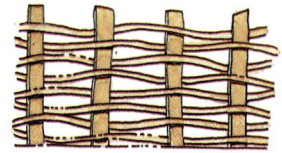

1. Wattles

2. Daubed with clay

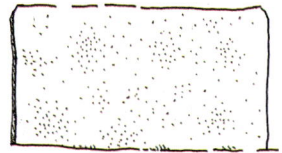

3. Plastered

4. Whitewashed

Above How to build a wall with wattle and daub. This method of building was used for many hundreds of years (and in some parts of the world it still is). It is cheaper and quicker than building in stone and relies on materials that are fairly common.

Right A selection of local building styles. See if you can find out about any others from your local library.

Local Building styles

Hebridean
black house

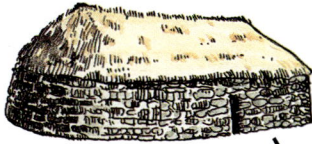

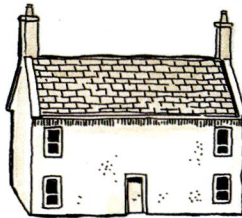

Scottish croft

Lakeland
farmhouse

brick nogging
and thatch

Yorkshire
gritstone
cottage

carstone,
cottage,
West
Norfolk

Irish long-house

Kent
weatherboarding

black-and-white
"magpie" house,
Cheshire

round house,
Cornwall

Somerset cob
and thatch

Cotswold
limestone

4 Change

You have now taken a good look at your neighbourhood as it is at present. What was it like in the past? What changes have occurred? Can you remember any that have happened in your lifetime? Perhaps some old buildings have been pulled down and replaced by new ones, or perhaps they have been demolished to make space for a new road.

You now start your real exploration of the past. This is where you will need help and guidance from your parents or teachers, to get everything in the proper order. You will need a file or scrapbook in which to store all the information you already have or which you will be collecting.

Examining old photographs, drawings or paintings of your town can be a useful way of finding out how its appearance has changed. Below is a picture of central Brighton at the turn of the century . . .

...and here is how that scene looks today. The clock tower remains, but the Lion Hotel behind it has been replaced by a large modern store. Traffic lights and telephone boxes have appeared. Make a list of the differences between the two pictures.

Do you have a family album of photographs? If so, see if you can find in it any pictures of your neighbourhood in the past. Visit your local library. There will probably be a section relating to local history, where you will find more pictures. There will also be old maps, which you can compare with up-to-date ones of your area.

Talk about your neighbourhood in the past with your parents, grandparents and elderly neighbours. You will find that they will tell you not only what changes have occurred, but why they have happened as well. Perhaps a row of buildings was destroyed by bombs during a war, or perhaps a new industrial site has grown up where houses once stood. Our surroundings change to meet the changing needs of people.

Above A scene from one of York's narrow streets. In the Middle Ages the growth of many towns was restricted by lack of space within the town walls, so buildings had to be built closer and closer together. This produced the narrow streets with over-hanging storeys which can still be seen in some places today.

House styles

The age of a house can often be guessed after a careful look at its style of building. In the past, as today, builders followed the latest fashions when designing houses. For instance, sash windows were introduced towards the end of the seventeenth century, and they became a desirable feature in houses built after this period. As it often took many years for new ideas to reach the provinces, similar building styles in different parts of the country are not necessarily from exactly the same period.

In the Middle Ages most towns were enclosed by a strong wall to keep out enemies. The space inside the wall was usually very limited, so houses had to be crammed into every available space, sometimes so close that their overhanging upper stories almost touched each other over the narrow streets.

Tudor, Elizabethan and early Jacobean houses of the sixteenth and early seventeenth centuries have distinctive and easily recognizable brickwork and timberwork. The use of timber frames is typical, but beware of modern imitations.

Houses of the Queen Anne and Georgian periods (early eighteenth century) are often

Tudor

Queen Anne

Georgian

distinguished by hipped roofs and large blocks of stone on the corners of the walls.

The main characteristics of the Regency style (named after the Prince Regent, 1811–1830) are elegant terraced houses, crescents, wrought-iron railings, balconies and bow windows.

In early industrial towns, rows of houses were often built back to back, with no yards, back doors or gardens. The reason for this was the need to house workers within walking distance of their place of work, combined with a severe lack of building space.

The Victorian era saw the development of housing for the masses. The main house-type for the Victorian worker was the terraced house, while houses for the well-to-do were often elaborate and ornate, with features copied from churches of the Gothic period.

The twentieth century has seen an improvement in housing for the ordinary person. Edwardian houses, with bay windows, were a development of the late Victorian styles. After the First World War, houses became plainer in appearance. Some experiments were made with concrete and flat roofs, and semi-detached houses became increasingly popular.

Above Victorian terraced houses in Newcastle.

Below Examples of some architectural styles which you may find in your town or neighbourhood.

Edwardian   1930s Semi-detached   1980s Detached

13

After the Second World War, there was a further move towards greater simplicity of design, with plain, unadorned fronts. Impressive attempts were made to provide many housing units in a limited space, by building tower-blocks. The idea was to relieve the housing shortage resulting from so many buildings having been destroyed by war-time bombing, at a time when building land was scarce. These tower-blocks, however, have not proved satisfactory, and some are now being demolished.

What examples can you find of different styles of architecture in your neighbourhood? Use the illustrations on these pages to help you. Turn back to page 7. See how the buildings you have listed there fit in with the styles of architecture we have mentioned. By recording where different styles occur you may be able to see how your town has grown through the ages.

Above Tower blocks such as this one were once thought to be the answer to the problem of housing shortage. **Below** Today, housing with fewer storeys is favoured.

5 Castles and forts

Castles are to be found in most parts of the British Isles. Like other types of buildings, they changed through the centuries as parts were added and others demolished.

Most castles date back to the period between the Norman Conquest in 1066 and the start of the fourteenth century. They usually occupy prominent sites: many were built to defend important road junctions or river crossings, and they also acted as places of refuge for people living locally when threatened by enemy invaders. People often built their homes as close to the castle walls as possible. In this way, many towns grew up around castles. Edinburgh is a fine example of a town built just outside the castle walls.

Edinburgh Castle dominates the town which has grown up around it.

Castles were also places from where a king or one of his lords could keep law and order over the surrounding area.

The term 'castle' should really be applied only to those buildings which were erected after the Normans invaded England in 1066. However, there are plenty of remains visible today of fortifications which were built before this date. For instance, you can still see the banks and ditches of ancient hill-forts, such as at Maiden Castle in Dorset; in Scotland there are many round towers, known as Brochs, built by the Celtic peoples; and along Hadrian's wall one can see the remains of Roman forts.

The earliest castles were called motte and bailey castles. They consisted of a circular mound of earth (a motte), topped by a strong wooden fence (a palisade) and a wooden tower. At the foot of the motte was a circular courtyard (a bailey) with a few buildings inside. This was surrounded by a ditch and another wooden fence. The motte was the strongest part of the castle.

Later, the towers and fences of these mottes were replaced by a circular stone wall, for greater protection. Various rooms were built inside this wall, with a small courtyard in the centre. This arrangement was called a shell keep. Later still, stone walls, known as curtain walls, were often built around the keep. Towers were added at intervals along the walls. At first these were square, but square towers and keeps proved to be weak at the corners. Attackers soon found that they could loosen stones or mine underneath to make part of the tower collapse. In time these were replaced with round designs.

Sometimes the inner walls and towers were built to overlook the curtain walls and its towers. Castles of this kind were known as concentric

Here is how one castle may have developed through the ages.

**About 1100
motte and bailey**

**About 1215
gateway, walls, chapel, great hall**

**About 1400
keep and tower**

Like many castles, Beaumaris, on the Isle of Anglesey, is today little more than a shell, although its massive walls are still intact. In fact, the castle was never fully completed. Work began in 1295 but stopped in 1330, due to lack of money.

castles. This meant that the defenders could fire more arrows at the attackers below.

If possible, the castle was encircled by a moat filled with water, and entry was by means of a drawbridge across the moat, which could be pulled up when necessary. Castles also had massive gates (portcullises) which could be shut fast at night, and strong gatehouses to protect them.

Here is an artist's impression of how Beaumaris would have looked if all the original plans had been carried out.

Living quarters

The castle keep was often where the castle's inhabitants lived. The first floor of the keep was the important one, the floor at ground level being occupied by workrooms, store-rooms and so on. Most of the space on the first floor was occupied by the great hall, where the king or lord conducted business, ate his meals and entertained his guests.

Most castles had a chapel, and sometimes there was a private chamber for the lord and his family. In early castles, however, he and his wife and children slept in an alcove in the thick walls. Later, the alcoves were enlarged into bedrooms. The servants simply slept on the floor of the great hall, as near to the fire as they could get in winter.

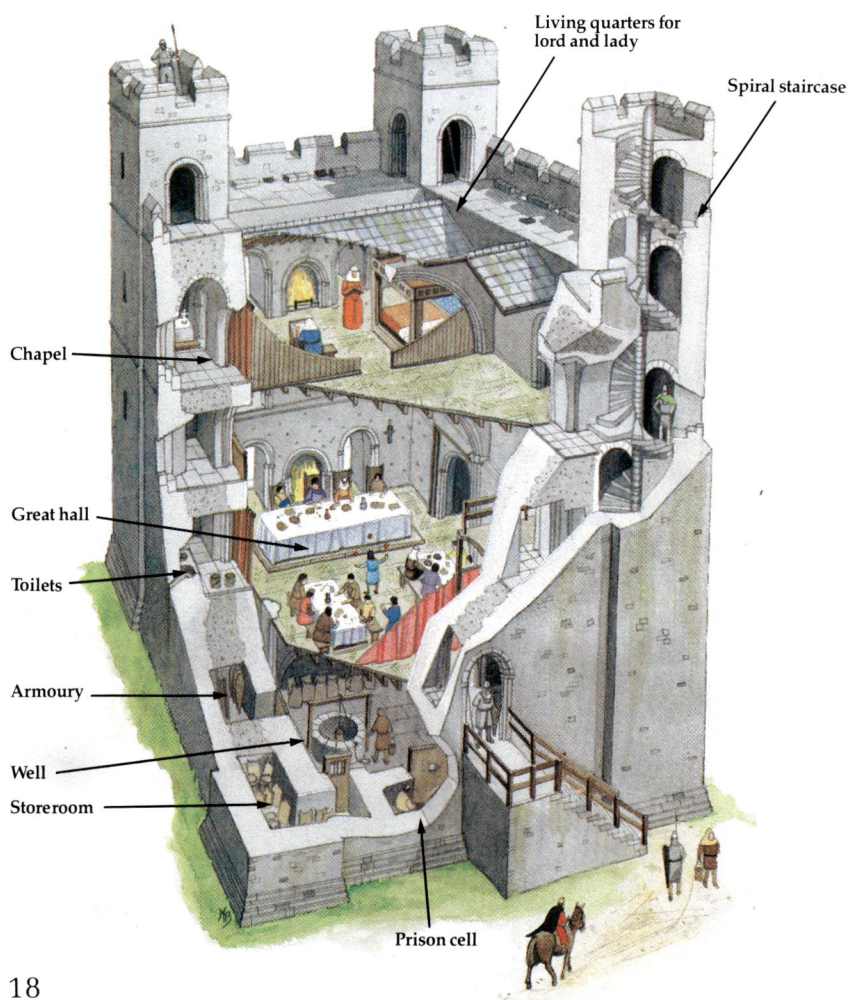

Living quarters for lord and lady

Spiral staircase

Chapel

Great hall

Toilets

Armoury

Well

Storeroom

Prison cell

Although many castles today look ruined and lifeless, they were once centres of much activity. This cutaway drawing shows what the interior of a castle keep may have looked like in the twelfth century.

castle features

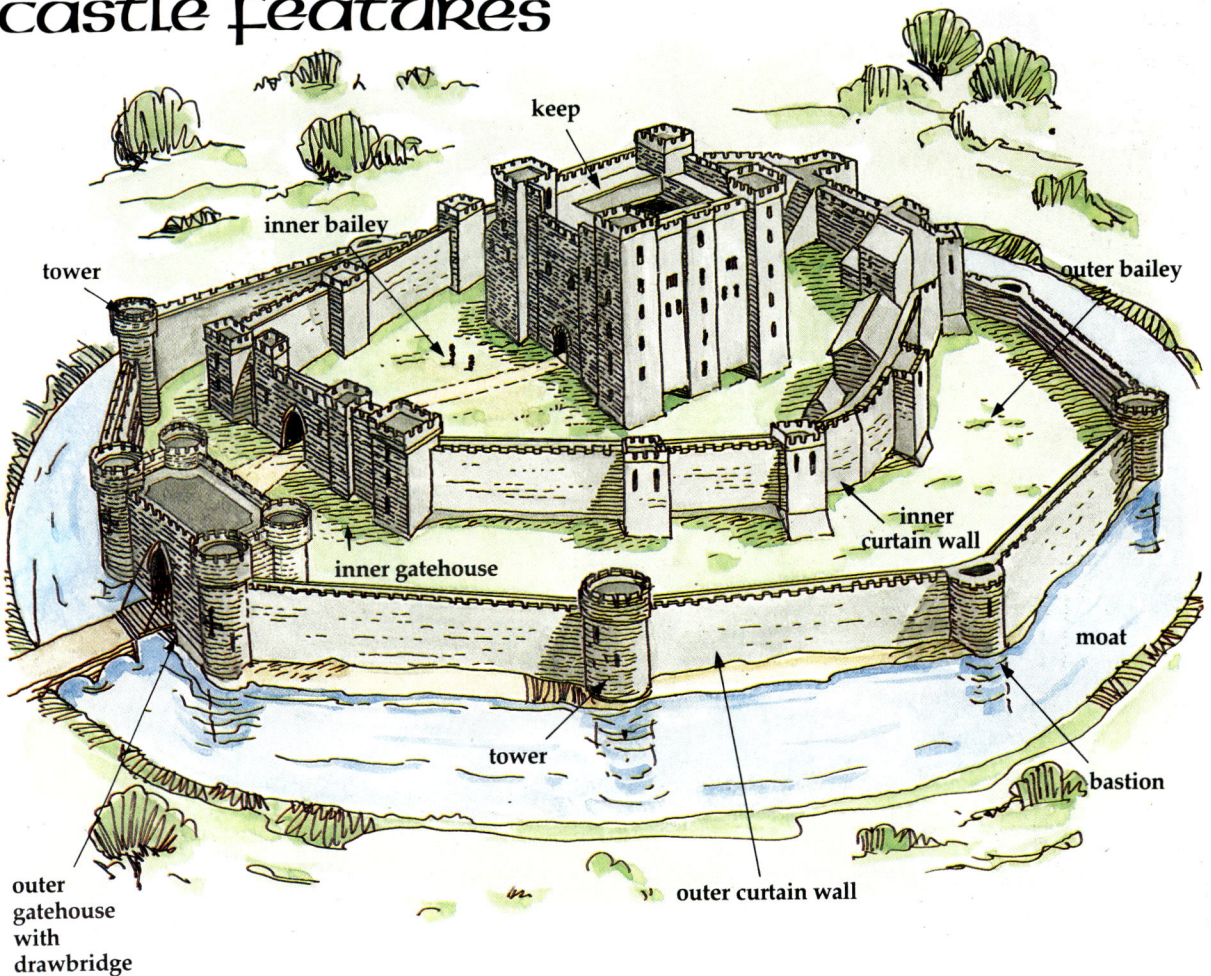

keep

inner bailey

tower

inner gatehouse

outer bailey

inner curtain wall

moat

tower

bastion

outer curtain wall

outer gatehouse with drawbridge

Visiting a castle

Many castles you visit will be in ruins. Try to picture what the castle might have looked like in its original state. Guide books often show artists' drawings of what the castle may have looked like at various points in history.

Look out for earth banks, ditches and moats to keep attackers away from the castle walls. Count the number of towers and arrow slits from where the defenders could fire arrows at their enemies. How high and how thick were the walls? Where do you think the castle's weakest point was? Imagine the dangers and difficulties you would face if you were a member of an attacking army.

Above Some features to look out for when you next visit a castle.
Below Two types of arrow slits. Sketch any others you find.

Once inside, look out for evidence of fireplaces, in the walls, drains and toilets (often just holes or shafts in the walls). Was there a chapel or church? Can you find kitchens, a great hall, dungeons or a well? If the castle's towers or keep are hollow, can you see the holes in the walls where wooden beams were inserted to support the floors above?

why Build here?

When you next visit a castle or fort (or indeed, any historical building) ask yourself why it was built in that particular spot. Here are a few questions which may help you find out:

- Is the site easy to reach?
- Is it near important roads?
- Is there a ready water supply?
- Were the building materials available locally?
- Is it built on a hill for protection?
- Was the site once linked to local farming or industry?
- Is it near a town or the coast?
- Did the castle defend a place where a river was crossed?

Imagine that you are going to build a castle. Find an Ordnance Survey map (either 1:25,000 or 1:50,000 scale), preferably of your area, but it is not that important. Choose a site to build your castle. Remember that you will need to be near a water supply, have good road communications and have building materials available locally. Your site will have to be easy to defend. Draw a plan of the area around your site. Draw in your castle and the things which influenced you to choose this site.

Above *Conwy Castle, in Wales, guards the entrance to the mouth of the River Conwy and the bridges which cross it. Always try to find out why a castle was built in a particular place.*

Below *Your own map will show not just your castle, but the things which helped you decide where to build it.*

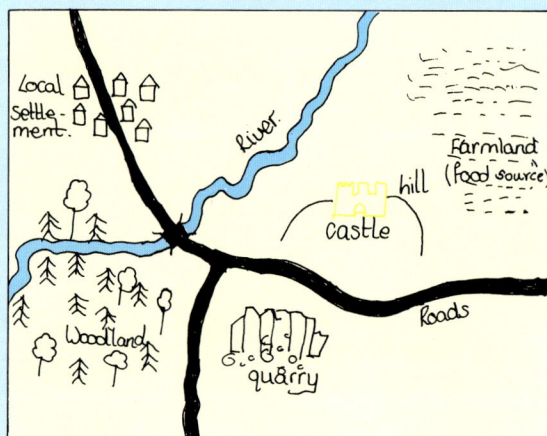

6 Religious buildings

In the past, religion formed a very important part of people's lives. Most villages had a church and castles had their own private chapels for worship.

Before Christianity came to Britain, people worshipped the gods which they believed lived in sacred streams, stones, pools and trees. Many Christian churches were later built on such sacred sites. Christians in those times thought it fitting to worship God in an imposing building at least as large as any other in the settlement.

In time, some of these parish churches grew into splendid cathedrals many of which are outstanding examples of different styles of architecture. Salisbury Cathedral (find Salisbury on a map of England) took nearly fifty years to build in the

Salisbury Cathedral, in Wiltshire, took nearly fifty years to complete.

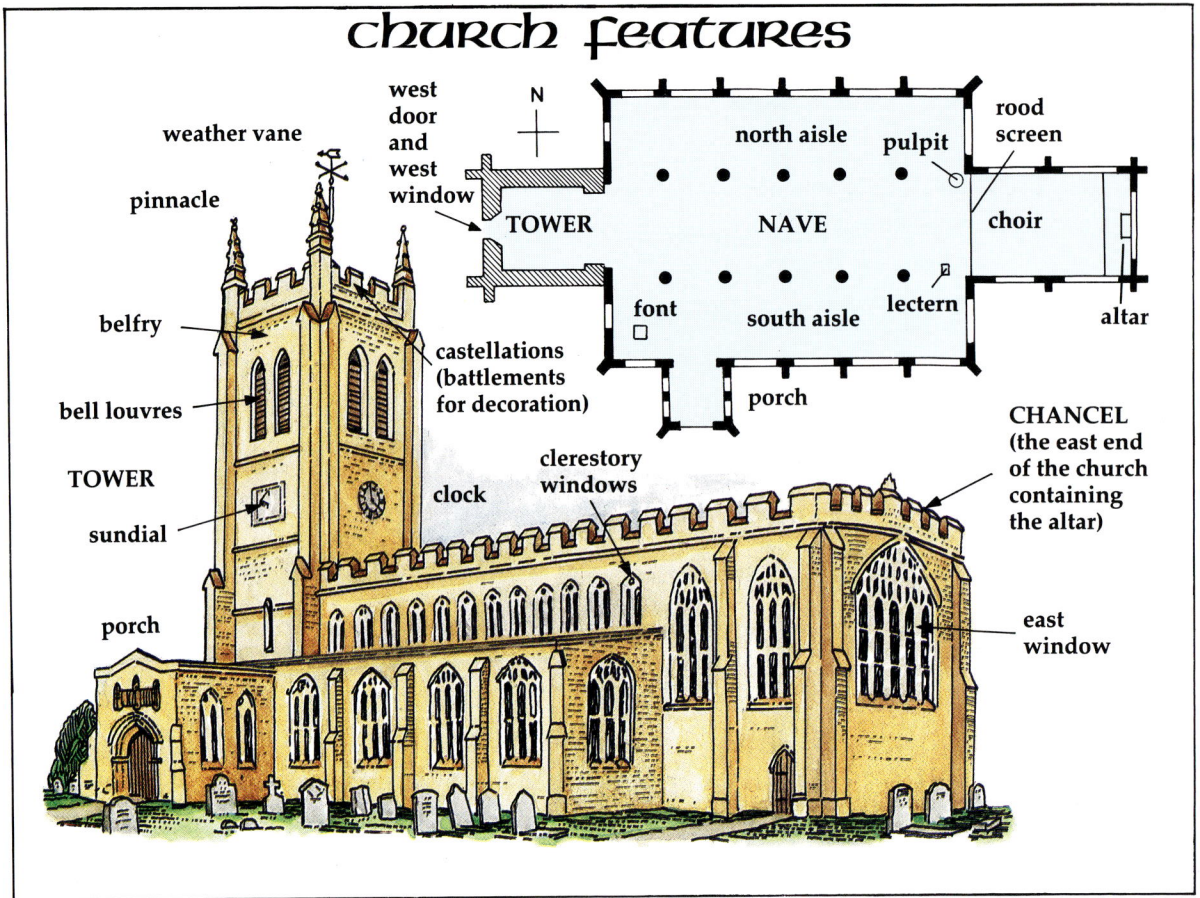

church features

weather vane

pinnacle

belfry

bell louvres

TOWER

sundial

porch

west door and west window

TOWER

castellations (battlements for decoration)

clerestory windows

clock

N

north aisle

NAVE

font

south aisle

pulpit

rood screen

choir

lectern

porch

altar

CHANCEL (the east end of the church containing the altar)

east window

thirteenth century and is a fine example of Gothic architecture. Its elegant spire, soaring to a height of 123m, was added later. In contrast, a peasant's hut at that time could have been built easily in four or five days.

Learn how to identify the different parts of a church. They include the nave, the chancel, the altar, the choir and the pulpit (see diagram).

Note that churches usually have the altar at the eastern end and the font, where babies are baptized, just inside the west door. An altar, where animals and sometimes even humans were sacrificed, was the chief feature of temples in pre-Christian times.

Altars are still prominent features in most Christian churches, though they are not, of

What to look for when you visit a typical parish church.

course, used for the same purpose! The altar is where Communion or Mass is celebrated, a central feature of Christian worship which commemorates Jesus' sacrifice of His life. You will find that each part of a religious building has a special purpose and meaning.

*Few old buildings that you see today look as they did when they were originally built. Most have gone through several changes. **Below left** How the church on page 22 might have developed over the centuries. **Below right** Some features to look out for inside a church.*

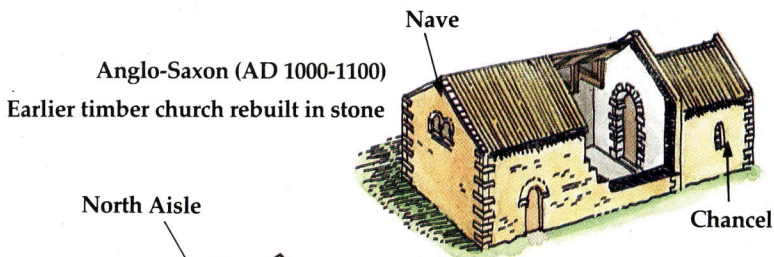

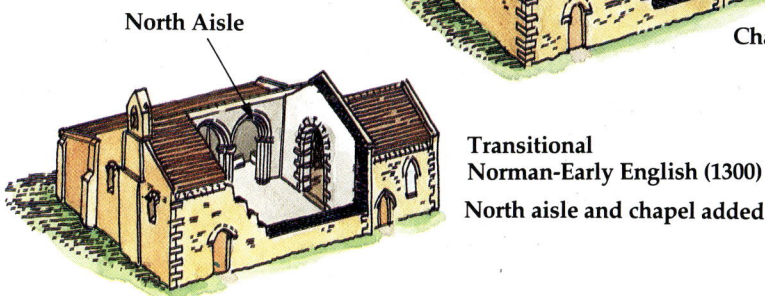

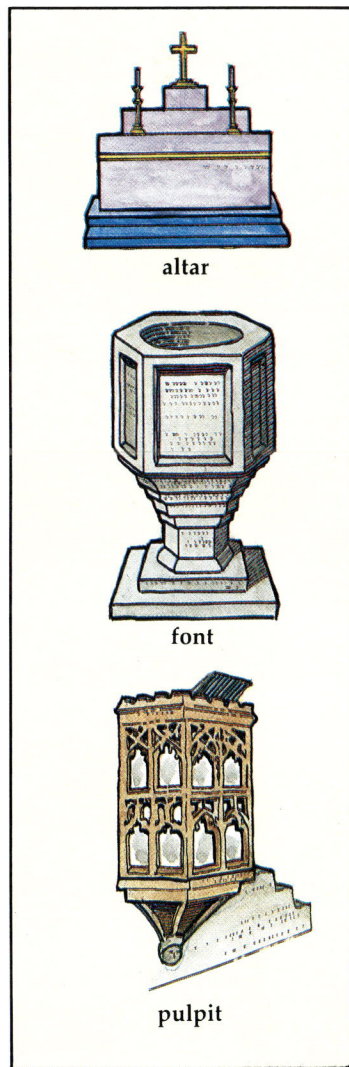

Anglo-Saxon (AD 1000-1100)
Earlier timber church rebuilt in stone

Nave

North Aisle

Chancel

Transitional
Norman-Early English (1300)
North aisle and chapel added

Early English
(1300-1400)
Nave and aisle lengthened; tower, porch and chapel added

Decorated (1450)
Chancel and tower enlarged and south aisle added

altar

font

pulpit

ɒevelopmenꞇ oꝼ ɑ pɑrish church

23

Visiting a local church

Local churches or chapels (or indeed any place of worship) can be useful places to find out about local history.

Look at the stained-glass windows in a local parish church. They create a soft, tinted light inside the building, but some also tell a story from the Bible or the lives of the saints. Hundreds of years ago they provided a visual lesson for worshippers in an age when few people could read. In some churches you will find old wall-paintings and carvings which served the same purpose. Modern stained-glass windows may be memorials to those people of the parish who died in the two World Wars.

In the Middle Ages it became fashionable to erect monumental brasses and inscribed tablets in churches in memory of important local people. These brasses and the carved stone figures on old tombs in churches, normally depict the person prepared for the grave, with hands together, limbs straightened and eyes gazing skywards. The

Above Many stained-glass windows bear dedications to local people or give the names of church benefactors.

Below Churches often contain the tombs of important figures in local history.

clothes they are wearing usually faithfully reproduce the costume of the period. These brasses or tombs may record the person's name, and you may find that some of the names are still known locally.

Similar information can be collected from gravestones in churchyards. What is the oldest inscription you can find in your local graveyard? What is the newest? Are there any unusual dedications on some of the stones (such as 'Here lies Ann Mann; she lived an old Maid and she died an old Mann!')?

Of course, not all places of worship belong to the Christian religion. In many towns and cities there are synagogues, where Jews worship. In the present century many mosques have been built by Muslims. There are temples, too, for people of many other religions, including Hindus, Sikhs and Buddhists. On a map of your town or neighbourhood, mark all the religious buildings, with a colour code for each religion. Do they follow any sort of pattern?

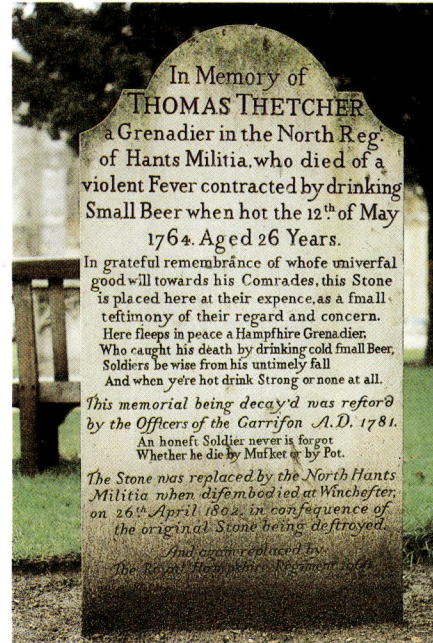

The 'Grenadier' tombstone in the grounds of Winchester Cathedral.

Below A mosque at Strathclyde in Glasgow. Although the oldest religious buildings you see will probably be of the Christian religion, there are many other religions practised in Britain today. Try to visit as many different places of worship as possible. Make a note of the main features, both inside and out. Do you notice any similarities between religious buildings of different faiths?

making a BRASS RUBBING

Thick wax crayons are best for making brass rubbings. You can get a variety of effects by using different colours or putting a water-colour wash over the rubbing. This enables you to add colour to the original design.

Let us assume that you want to take a rubbing from an old brass set into the floor of the church.

1. First, dust the brass lightly with a soft cloth, working from the centre towards the edges to remove any grit.

2. Cover the design with a sheet of paper and fix it in position by sticking down each corner with masking tape.

3. Feel for the edge of the brass and work the crayon across the paper with light strokes. Work from the top to bottom and take care not to scribble or tear the paper.

4. When you have been over the whole design, carefully remove the paper. Make sure that you leave the brass clean. Remember to make notes on the back of the rubbing, so that you have a record of the church in which you made it.

The same technique can be used to take rubbings of inscriptions, memorials and wall-plaques. Always ask the churchwarden for permission before you take a rubbing.

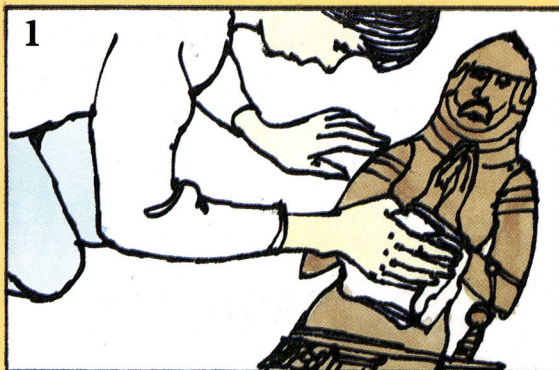

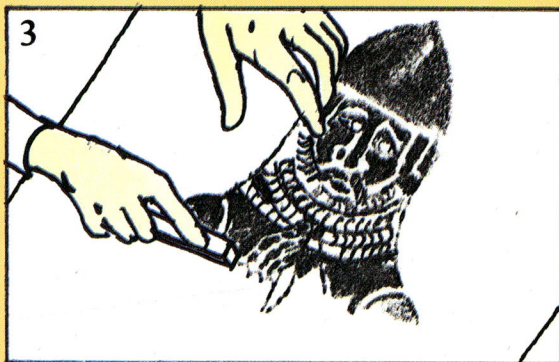

7 Shops and inns

Your parents may be able to remember when there were no supermarkets. That was not such a long time ago. Before supermarkets became widespread, shops tended to specialize in selling goods of one particular type. Bakers, butchers, grocers, greengrocers, ironmongers and so on, all had their own special shops.

Earlier still, there were no shops at all. Each little community produced most of the things it needed. From time to time, however, there were fairs or markets where things were exchanged. People came from miles around to buy and sell. See if you can find out whether any fairs or markets are held in your area, or whether there used to be any that have been discontinued.

A butcher's shop in 1943, quite different to the big, bright supermarkets where most families buy their meat today, in frozen or ready-packed portions. Note the meat hanging up outside the shop in the open air.

There are thousands of historic inns and public houses in Britain which date back many hundreds of years.

Shops came into being when people who made things wanted to show what they had for sale. They put their goods on display in the front windows of their houses, where passers-by could see them. Anyone needing, for instance, a pair of shoes could see them in the shoemaker's window and, peering in, could see the shoemaker at work on another pair. The family ate and lived in a back room and slept upstairs.

One of the many things people made in their houses was ale. Often customers who came to buy ale wanted to stay and drink it there, and travellers might want a meal or a bed for the night. So the ale-maker's house became an inn. As custom increased, so more and more rooms had to be added. In some of the older inns, by studying different styles of building and materials, you can see just how the buildings grew, with bits added at different times.

Make a note also of some local inn signs and their names. An inn may show a connection with a local industry, such as 'The Railway Tavern'. Or it may have connections with a famous person

A collection of local inn names may reveal connections with historical figures and events, or perhaps with industry or agriculture. When you note down the names of the inns, sketch the inn signs as well.

who lived locally, such as 'Lord Nelson's Arms'. It may even commemorate some historical event, such as 'The Royal Oak', which refers to the adventure of King Charles II who, after losing a battle, hid in an oak tree.

Many early schools started in private houses, too. Sometimes a widow would set up a little school in her home, charging a few pence a week. Such schools were known as Dame Schools.

You will find that in the course of time, buildings have often changed their uses. You may remember some changes in your own neighbourhood. Ask your grandparents or an elderly neighbour about such changes and study old photographs so that you can compare them with the present. You may find that an inn has become a shop, or an old town hall has become offices. A big house may now be a school, or an old people's home. Cinemas may even have become bingo halls.

A lesson in progress at a Dame School, 1887.

8 Public buildings

When people began to live in large communities, they needed special buildings where business affairs could be conducted. Disputes had to be heard by judges; criminals had to be tried and punished; taxes had to be collected. When the community was not very large, the business was usually dealt with in the house of the local chief. Sometimes it would be the king or queen of that region; sometimes a great lord. For that reason, many old castles and palaces had a great hall, into which a great number of people could crowd.

As Britain became more prosperous, particularly during the second half of the nineteenth century, most important towns built imposing civic and public buildings, such as town halls (in Scotland, town houses), courts of justice, new schools, museums, hospitals, police stations, public baths, libraries and so on.

The Public Record Office at Kew in London. The public buildings of today have a much different appearance, and often completely different uses, from those of the past.

The old town hall at Wootton Bassett in Wiltshire, now restored to its original condition, was built in the seventeenth century.

What public buildings are there in your town? Some may be relatively new; others may be older and bear commemorative plaques telling when the building was first built or who opened it. Make a list of civic and public buildings in your area and try to find out when they were built. Mark them on the map you have already made of your neighbourhood. You will probably find that there are some types of public buildings which did not exist in the past, such as sports centres and community centres. Why do you think this is so?

Many fine public buildings were constructed during the nineteenth century, as Britain became more prosperous. The Natural History Museum in London is an excellent example.

9 Stately homes

What is the difference between your house and, for instance, Buckingham Palace in London, or The White House in Washington? Those buildings are very much larger, and they reflect the importance of the positions held by the people who live there. In the past, though not always today, people have tended to live in as large a house as they could afford. So a house could tell you a lot about the people who lived there.

The stately homes and historic houses of England, Scotland, Wales and Ireland are remarkable places, beautiful to look at and exciting to explore. Many of them are open to the public and many have fine gardens.

When you next visit a historic house, try to find out about the people who originally built it. Try also to imagine what sort of everyday life they led. Can you imagine what life was like for children growing up in the house? Look out for different styles of furniture, paintings, tapestries, ornate decoration and so on. Make a note of how the house was lit and heated. How did these houses compare to those of ordinary people?

Design your own stately home and its formal gardens. Imagine that you have as much money and whatever building materials you need at your disposal. What rooms would you include which you do not have in your own house or flat?

Right Blickling Hall in Norfolk, one of the National Trust's many properties open to the public. The present building, an impressive red-brick house of the seventeenth century, stands on the site of an earlier house built in 1390.

10 Industry

As new industries develop, so new types of buildings are created to cater for them. Two hundred years ago the Industrial Revolution in Britain began because the population was increasing fast and so creating a demand for more goods. It was based on a new source of power – steam from coal – which, together with the invention of new machines, made possible greatly-increased production.

Craftsmen who had previously made goods in their own front rooms or workshops now found that they had to move into vast new factories where they could make use of the new machinery. Many industries became localized. This was partly due to the availability of raw materials, but even more important were the advantages of being near a source of coal and iron.

Woollen goods, for instance, which used to be knitted in cottages in many parts of England, became concentrated into factories in Bradford

The visible remains of a redundant tin mine in Cornwall.

and other towns in Yorkshire. Yorkshire had not only plenty of sheep to produce the wool but also an abundant supply of coal. On the other side of the Pennines, the towns of Lancashire became noted for cotton goods, because the climate is so damp that cotton thread, imported from America via Liverpool, could be used without fear of it breaking. Nottingham specialized in making stockings and lace; Leicester in boots and shoes.

Of course, many of the new industries required buildings specially suited to their needs. Coalmines needed surface buildings and great wheels for bringing up coal and miners from deep down.

Disused brick kilns at Stoke. There are many reminders like this of industry in the past. What old industrial sites are there in your town?

In Cornwall, derelict stone towers mark the sites of once flourishing tin-mines, now disused. Many old industrial buildings have now acquired new uses: factories and warehouses may have been transformed into shopping arcades or flats.

Now a new industrial revolution is in progress. Many old heavy industries are dying out and small airy factories on new estates are taking their place. There, highly skilled workers make parts for electronic equipment, computers and other intricate machines. Also relatively new are electricity generating stations, chemical plants, oil refineries and modern sewage works.

What industrial buildings are there in your town or district? Are the local industries different from those of the past? What evidence can you find of former industries? What differences do you notice between the industrial buildings of today and those of the past?

These eighteenth-century warehouses at St Katharine's Dock in London have now been converted into a shopping and leisure area.

A factory unit on a modern industrial estate in Macclesfield. Compare this picture with pictures you can find of factories at the turn of the century or even earlier. How do you think working conditions have changed since those days?

11 | Place names

When exploring the past, place names and street names can be a great help and supply us with a lot of useful clues.

For instance, Doncaster grew up around a fort by the river Don ('caster' being derived from the Latin *castrum*, meaning a fortified place. The word 'chester', often found in place names, also comes from *castrum*). There are scores of mill towns or Miltons (in Gaelic, *Baile a' Mhuilinn*), many of which bear traces of a mill.

It is tempting to guess at the origin of a name, but beware of jumping to conclusions. The derivation of the name Bridgewater would seem to be obvious, as it is built on the site of a bridge across a river mouth in Somerset. However, the name is actually derived from 'Burgh Walter', which means 'Walter's Town'!

Place names can also contain elements of more than one language. The basic language in England is Anglo-Saxon, or English, but in Wales, Scotland and Ireland many place names preserve the original languages of Welsh, Gaelic and Irish respectively. The word 'ford' in a place name usually indicates that a river could be crossed by wading (Bedford is an example). But in Waterford, in Ireland, 'ford' is derived from the Viking (Norse) word 'fjord', meaning a deep sea-inlet.

Perhaps your part of the town where you live has a separate name from the town itself. This usually indicates that it was once a separate village which has been swallowed-up as the town grew. Try to find the meanings of some of the more important local names.

Many towns and villages which grew up around mills like the one below, now bear the name Milton.

street names

We are all familiar with the name 'High Street', which usually referred to the main street of a town or village. Here are some categories into which we can divide street names:

1. Those relating to physical features, such as Hill Street or Elm Tree Lane.
2. Names connected with work or industry, such as Brick-kiln Lane or Butcher Row.
3. Those with church or religious associations, such as St Peter's Street or Trinity Lane.
4. Former land uses, such as Meadow Lane or Silver Road (a reminder of Roman times, since *silva* is Latin for 'wood').
5. Fairs and markets, such as Cheese Market or Yarn Market.
6. Former town features, such as Well Place or White Hall.
7. Important local people, such as Latimer Crescent or King Alfred Square.
8. Legends, such as Giant's Hill or Dragon's Lane.
9. Transport, such as Bridge Street or Great Western Road (referring to the Great Western Railway).

Look at the street names opposite. Try to fit them into the categories we have mentioned. Make a list of the street names in your locality, particularly the older streets. Do they fit into these categories? What do they tell you about local history? Does it confirm what you have already found out about your neighbourhood?

CHURCH LANE

Goose Acre

Corn Market

The Stocks

VICTORIA PLACE

CANAL WAY

Druids Corner

Oaklands

Candlemakers Row

12 Archaeology

Above *At an archaeological dig, every square metre of soil is examined in the search for evidence of the past.*

If your town has existed for many centuries, very few (if any) of the original buildings will still be standing. Even castles and palaces may have disappeared, and certainly the houses of ordinary people will have done so.

Often a site will have been used many times. When a building was demolished, the materials of which it was made were often used to build another on the same site. Archaeologists exploring the past by digging find many layers of material, each layer consisting of the remains of earlier buildings.

As town centres are developed, 'rescue digs' are frequently going on. Find out if any are in progress in your town. They happen when a site is cleared for a new building, and archaeologists excavate in order to discover what the site has been used for in the past.

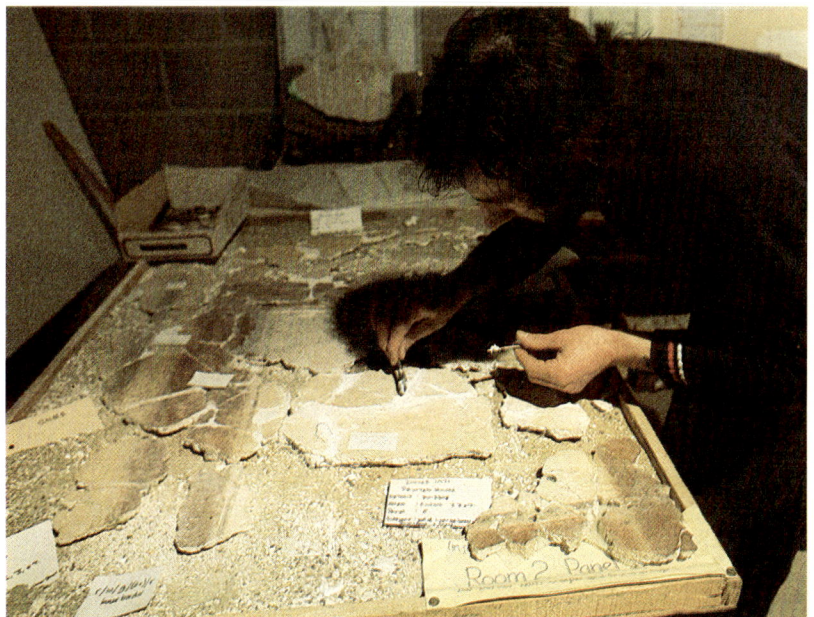

Left *An archaeologist carefully tries to piece together the remains of an ancient wall-painting.*

Archaeological investigation enables us to build up a picture of what everyday life was like for people in past ages. At the Jorvik Viking Centre, in York, an entire Viking village has been reconstructed.

Archaeologists usually only have a short time to conduct their excavations before the site is covered again and a new building rises on it. All that they have found, however, is carefully recorded and the most important finds are kept in the local museum. Try to visit your local museum and find out what the archaeologists have discovered about your area.

During their excavations, the archaeologists examine every spoonful of soil and every broken stone, marking exactly the place where it was found. All the information they have discovered is gathered together to create a picture of what life was like in certain periods of history. At the Jorvik Viking Centre, York, a Viking settlement has been reconstructed as it was a thousand years ago. Walking through it, you can see the families of that period going about their everyday life. You can even smell the roast cooking!

At Butser Hill, near Petersfield, Hampshire, an Iron Age farm has been reconstructed. Work is at present going on at a number of other similar projects. Perhaps you are fortunate enough to be within travelling distance of one such scheme.

13 | A local project

A local project will be about the buildings, past and present, in your area. Define carefully the area you are exploring. If you are working alone, do not make the area too large. It is better to collect a lot of details about a rather small area. If the project is to be undertaken by a class, however, it presents an excellent opportunity to work in pairs or in small groups. That way an entire town centre or village can be covered. Everything that the groups record should be entered on a plan of the area and discussed in class.

Keep the information you gather in a loose leaf folder. Use a separate page or two for each century. Include any maps or plans you have made. The earliest entries will be about what your locality was like before there were any buildings at all. Have your enquiries given you any clues? Was it forest country, marshland or a grassy plain? Use old maps, records and place names to help you.

As you use all the information you have gathered in a project about your area, you will begin to get a clearer picture of how it has changed over the years.

Fleet Street in London is now the headquarters of the British newspaper industry, but underneath all the buildings the River Fleet, a tributary of the Thames, still flows. Remember that climate, like everything else, changes. Land that is now dry ground may once have been a swamp. Much of Britain was once well-wooded. With all the information you have collected, try drawing a picture of the countryside on which your town or village is built before people began to move into the area.

London's Fleet Street. Below this busy street, the River Fleet still flows.

What next?

By the time you have finished your project the beginning of it will already be in the past. Perhaps some of the buildings you have described will have been demolished or perhaps new parts will have been added to existing buildings and others will have acquired new uses.

You may like to think about the changes which will occur in your area during the next five or ten years. Or perhaps even the next fifty years. At this stage, it can be helpful for visits to be

Left *If there is any demolition work in progress in your area, try to find out what buildings (if any) are going to take the place of those being knocked down. You may be able to find out from your local newspaper, or there may be a notice outside the site. Never enter a demolition site, as they are very dangerous places.*

arranged to the offices of the local planning authorities, of the public health inspector and of local architects and building authorities. From them you will learn their ideas about how your area is likely to develop over the coming years.

Back at school or at home, think about what you have seen. Discuss it with your group, friends or parents. Do you think the official plans for your area are adequate? Or do you think they should be altered in some way? Have you discovered a lack of amenities that ought to be put right? Are there, for instance, enough playing fields or enough housing for the elderly? Do the plans you know about involve destroying some things that you think ought to be preserved?

Your exploration of the past is beginning to produce results. It is making you think about the future. Nearly all the changes that have occurred to your area in the past have been made by people, just as the changes in the future will be. And remember – you will be one of the people who will make those changes.

Above *Investigate the plans for the future of your area. You may find that there is a lack of amenities, such as children's play areas.*
Below *Plans for a Scottish Exhibition and Cultural Centre in Glasgow. Are there any important projects planned for your area?*

Interviews and visits

Always make careful preparations before you pay a visit to a museum or an office and before you go to interview someone. You will find most people are helpful but remember that they may well be busy people, so do not waste their time. Be sure to take a pen or pencil and a notebook or paper on a clipboard. If you have a tape-recorder it will be very useful for interviewing.

Above all, make up your mind beforehand exactly what you want to find out. Prepare a list of questions, but do not try to cover too much ground at one interview.

Supposing you are going to interview a man who has lived in your town for sixty years. Try to avoid asking questions like, 'Please tell me what things were like fifty years ago.' If you decide that you want to know in what ways the town's High Street has changed, make a list of the buildings there now and ask him about each of them in turn. Ask questions like, 'When you were a boy, was W H Smith's at the corner?' He may remember that it was then a bicycle shop, where he bought his first bicycle. Remember not to ask too many questions, though!

Places to visit

In your exploration of the past, there are plenty of places you will be able to visit, although you may need to ask permission first. Here are a few ideas:

● your local library;
● your local museum and record office;
● the offices of your local newspaper; their files will contain much useful information, though you will need some guidance in your search and you should go equipped

with specific questions;
● any local civic buildings, such as a town hall or town house;
● churches or places of worship;
● industrial buildings;
● castles, stately homes, city/town walls, old inns or almshouses;
● your local planning office.

Take notice of similar features when you travel or go on holiday. Find out if there is a local archaeological or historical society. Try to obtain some of their publications.

Further reading

Allen, Eleanor, *Civic Pride* (A&C Black, 1979)
Allen, Eleanor, *Industry* (A&C Black, 1977)
Allen, Eleanor, *Market Towns* (A&C Black, 1979)
Davison, Brian K., *The Observers Book of Castles* (Warne, 1979)
Dunning, Robert, *Local Sources for the Young Historian* (Muller, 1973)
Hammersley, Alan, *Towns and Town Life* (Blandford, 1973)
Ingram, Tony, *Buildings* (Wayland, 1985)
Moss, Peter, *Town Life Through the Ages* (Harrap, 1972)
Pluckrose, Henry, *Churches* (Mills and Boon, 1977)
Pluckrose, Henry, *Seen in Britain* (Mills and Boon, 1977)
Woodlander, David and Brown, Judith, *Castles* (A&C Black, 1983)
Woodlander, David, and Brown, Judith, *Churches* (A&C Black, 1983)

The National Trust publishes a booklet *Properties Open*, which lists all the properties it maintains. It is available from any National Trust shop, or from the following address: The National Trust, 36 Queen Anne's Gate, London SW1. The National Trust for Scotland produces the following publications: *A Guide to over 100 Properties* and an *Educational Guide to the National Trust for Scotland*. Both are available from the Trust's headquarters at 5 Charlotte Street, Edinburgh EH2 4DU.

Glossary

Alcove   A recess in a wall of a room.

Altar   A flat-topped block or table on which offerings or sacrifices are offered to a god.

Amenities   Useful facilities or services to the local community.

Archaeology   A study of the past made by investigating objects, often by digging, rather than by reading history.

Bailey   The outer courtyard or enclosed area of a castle, surrounded by defensive stone walls, wooden fences and often ditches and banks.

Bay window   A window projecting from a wall and forming an alcove in a room.

Bow window   A bay window in the shape of a curve.

Broch   A circular dry-stone tower, large enough to be used as a fortified refuge for local people in times of danger. A great number of Brochs were built during the first century AD.

Chancel   The part of a church, near the altar, usually reserved for the clergy and choir.

Choir   The part of a church where the choir sits.

Civic   Relating to a city, town or its inhabitants. Civic buildings usually deal with local administration, recreation and so on.

Curtain wall   A wall around the outside of a castle, serving as a first line of defence.

Demolish   To destroy or pull down.

Excavate   To uncover buried remains by digging.

Font   A basin, usually of stone, holding water for baptism.

Gothic   A style of architecture, based on the use of pointed arches.

Hipped roof   A roof with sloping sides and ends.

Horizontal   Flat, level.

Hurdle   A framework of interwoven branches.

Industrial Revolution   The transformation in the eighteenth and nineteenth centuries of Britain (and later other Western European countries and the US) into industrial nations.

Keep   The main tower within the walls of a medieval castle or fortress.

Lintel   A horizontal post or stone forming the top part of a doorway.

Moat   A deep, wide ditch, generally filled with water, surrounding a castle or house.

Monumental brass   A memorial tablet of metal, on the wall of a church.

Mosque   A Muslim place of worship.

Motte   A mound of earth on which a castle was erected.

Nave   The part of a church generally occupied by worshippers.

Neolithic times   The period in history which was characterized by primitive farming methods and the use of flint tools (4000 to 2400 BC in Europe; 9000 to 6000 BC in south-west Asia).

Palisade   A fence of wooden stakes, especially for defence purposes.

Plaque   An ornamental tablet, usually commemorating a person, and fastened to a wall.

Portcullis   A sort of sliding gate, in the form of an iron or wooden grating which hung vertically in the gatehouse of a castle and which could be lowered to bar the entrance.

Pulpit   A raised platform from which a preacher delivers a sermon.

Quarry   A place where stone is dug for building.

Rescue dig   An archaeological excavaton undertaken on a site needed for building.

Sacred   Holy; dedicated to the worship of God or gods.

Sacrifice   An offering to God or to gods (especially on an altar).

Sash windows   A window with panes of glass which slide up and down.

Synagogue   A Jewish place of worship.

Terrace   A row of houses joined together.

Tributary   A stream that flows into another larger one.

Wattle and daub   A method of building by plastering interwoven twigs or branches with mud, clay or dung and straw.

Index

Picture Acknowledgements

The publishers would like to thank the following for supplying pictures: Aldus Archive 5 (top), 6, 14 (top), 19 (top and bottom), 39 (top) David Armitage 20 (bottom); Mark Bergin 18; Brighton Resort Services 11; British Tourist Authority 12 (top), 20 (middle), 25 (bottom), 42 (top), 43 (bottom); DP Press 26; The Mansell Collection 29; National Trust 24 (top), 32/33, 37; TOPHAM 4, 13 (top), 14 (bottom), 21, 25 (top), 27, 28 (bottom), 30 (top), 34, 35, 36 (bottom), 39 (bottom), 42 (bottom); Malcolm S Walker 38; Stephen Wheele 7 (top and bottom), 8, 9, 12 (bottom), 13 (bottom), 16, 19 (top and bottom), 20 (top), 22, 23, 41; Tim Woodcock *cover*, 24 (bottom), 28 (top), 30 (bottom), 31, 36 (top), 43 (top). All other pictures are from the Wayland picture library.